GOAL!

Peter Millett
Mal Chambers

nathan
10

Rigby

www.Rigby.com
1-800-531-5015

Rigby Focus Forward

This Edition © 2009 Rigby, a Harcourt Education Imprint

Published in 2008 by Nelson Australia Pty Ltd ACN: 058 280 149
A Cengage Learning company

1 2 3 4 5 6 7 8 374 14 13 12 11 10 09 08 07
Printed and bound in China

Goal!
ISBN-13   978-1-4190-3845-7
ISBN-10   1-4190-3845-1

GOAL!

Peter Millett
Mal Chambers

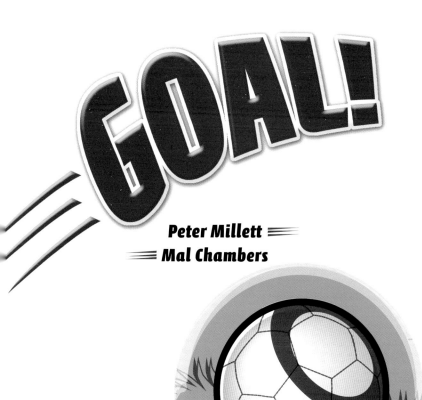

Contents

Chapter 1 **Nathan** 4

Chapter 2 **Learning Sign Language** 12

Chapter 3 **Soccer Skills** 16

Chapter 4 **End of the Game** 22

Nathan

Jeffrey and his friend Nathan raced toward the soccer field. Jeffrey looked worried. He was late for the game. Mr. Andrews, his coach, tapped his wrist like he was tapping a watch.

"Sorry we're late, Coach," said Jeffrey, puffing.

"That's OK," grumbled Coach Andrews.
"Get your shoes on—we're playing in
two minutes."

"I need to tell you something important
about my friend Nathan, Coach," said
Jeffrey, pulling his shoes on.

"Well, hurry up. What is it?" asked
Coach Andrews, looking over at
Nathan who was quickly tying his
shoes.

"Nathan is deaf," replied Jeffrey.

"He's what?" bellowed Coach Andrews.

"It won't be a problem. He's a really
awesome player—you'll see,"
Jeffrey said.

Coach Andrews shook his head. "Jeffrey, why didn't you tell me that yesterday? I could have found someone else to play for us instead. A deaf player won't fit into our team."

"Yes, he will," said Jeffrey. "You don't need to be able to hear to play soccer."

"Well, we'll see about that," replied Coach Andrews.

Goal!

Then the referee blew his whistle
and play started. Jeffrey and Nathan
rushed out onto the field while Coach
Andrews stood on the sideline.

Right away Nathan pounced on a
loose ball in midfield. Skillfully he
dribbled it toward the center line.

"Pass it to me!" screamed Jason, the winger running to his left. But Nathan kept on dribbling the ball up the middle of the field. Suddenly he was tackled from behind and lost possession. "Oh, man," groaned Jason.

Coach Andrews threw his hands up in the air in frustration. Jeffrey kept his head down low to avoid his glare.

A few moments later, Jeffrey sprinted down the touchline and won the ball back with a tackle. He spotted Nathan in the clear and signed him.

Nathan sprinted out toward the wing. Jeffrey kicked the ball high and wide over the defenders' heads. But suddenly there was a tweet as the referee blew his whistle.

"Offside!" the referee shouted.

However, Nathan didn't hear the referee's whistle and kept charging with the ball at his feet.

He ran at the goalkeeper and blasted the ball high into the back of the net. Nathan punched the air to celebrate scoring.

No one else in his team celebrated, and Coach Andrews let out another loud groan from the sideline.

Chapter 2

Learning Sign Language

At half time, Coach Andrews ran onto the field. "Jeffrey, I told you it wouldn't work—Nathan isn't fitting into our team!" he said.

But Jeffrey didn't say a word. He turned around and called all of his teammates into a huddle.

"OK, everyone, listen up. Nathan is deaf," Jeffrey said. "He can't hear you or the referee calling out to him. So we have to communicate with him using sign language. If the referee blows his whistle and stops play, show Nathan this sign …" Jeffrey chopped his right hand down on top of his left palm to show his teammates the sign language signal for "stop."

Jeffrey then showed his teammates some other hand signals to help them communicate

with Nathan on the field.

"We can do this," cried Jeffrey.

All of the players put their hands together in a circle and let out a loud "Hooagh!" Then the referee blew his whistle, and the second half started.

Almost immediately, one of Jeffrey's teammates was fouled by a sliding tackle from behind.

"Peep!" the referee's whistle blew loud and clear.

Eric, the captain, signed to Nathan to let him know to stop running. Nathan quickly stopped in his tracks. He smiled and signed back to Eric to thank him.

Jeffrey looked over at Coach Andrews. He noticed a small smile starting to slowly lift up his heavy frown.

Soccer Skills

As the second half went on, Jeffrey's teammates became more comfortable using sign language to communicate with Nathan. The more they included Nathan in the game, the better he played.

Coach Andrews was amazed by
Nathan's soccer skills. He had never
seen anyone dribble the ball with such
speed and precision before. When
Nathan glided across the grass, he
looked as though he was running with
the ball glued to his foot.

As the game neared its end, the scores were tied one-to-one. Coach Andrews watched anxiously as his team launched attack after attack on the other team's defense. Suddenly Jeffrey dribbled the ball between two defenders. He saw Nathan wide open. He signed to Nathan to tell him he was going to pass the ball.

Nathan took off like a rocket.
Jeffrey passed the ball high and wide
out toward the right wing. Holding his
whistle between his lips, the referee
watched the ball fly through the air.

But Nathan was onside. He dodged a diving tackle from behind, then raced toward the goalkeeper. He cut around the goalkeeper and hammered the ball high up into the net. Nathan jumped in the air and punched the sky with delight.

This time everyone on his team jumped up and celebrated as well.

"Whoohoo!" cheered Jeffrey.

Chapter 4

End of the Game

Nathan was swamped by a sea of yellow shirts. "You did it—you did it—you won us the game!" bellowed Jeffrey.

The referee looked down at his watch and blew his whistle to signal the end of the game.

Coach Andrews rushed onto the field sporting a beaming smile. "Jeffrey, what can I say?" he said loudly. "I was wrong and you were right. Nathan fit into our team perfectly!"

"Don't worry about it, Coach," Jeffrey said, smiling.

Coach Andrews jogged over to Nathan and patted him on the back. He didn't say a word to Nathan—he just gave him a friendly hand signal that he knew everyone else on the team was sure to understand!